NATURE

Written by Olivia Watson
Illustrated by Tjarda Borsboom

First published in 2025 by Hungry Tomato Ltd.
F15, Old Bakery Studios, Blewetts Wharf,
Malpas Road, Truro, Cornwall, TR1 1QH, UK.

Thanks to our creative team:
Editors: Holly Thornton and Jenny Rowan
Designers: Amy Harvey and Meg Holbrook

Copyright © 2025 Hungry Tomato Ltd

Beetle Books is an imprint of Hungry Tomato.

No part of this publication may be reproduced, stored in a retrieval system, or transmitted in any form or by any means, electronic, mechanical, photocopying, recording, or otherwise, without prior written permission of the copyright owner. A CIP catalog record for this book is available from the British Library.

ISBN: 9781916598652

Printed and bound in China

Discover more at
www.hungrytomato.com

Contents

What Is Nature?	8	Ancient Plants	24
Planet Earth	10	Tree Communication	26
Moving Surfaces	12	Amazing Plant Adaptations	28
Under the Surface	14	What Am I?	30
What's Hidden Inside Rocks?	16	Keeping the Planet Healthy	32
The Water Cycle	18	Types of Animals	34
Beyond Earth	20	Clever Animal Adaptations	36
How Plants Grow	22	Incredible Insects	38

Words in **BOLD** can be found in the glossary.

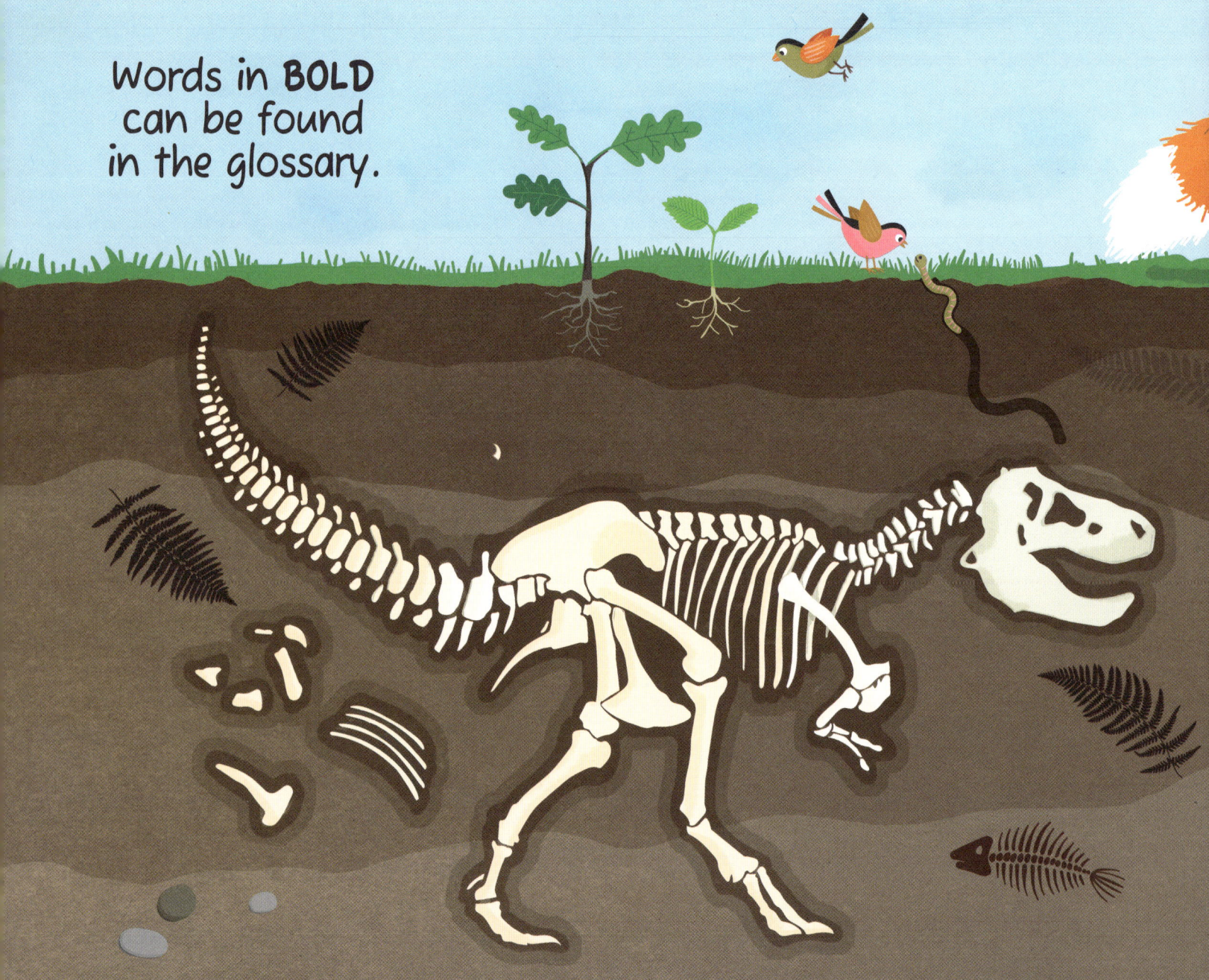

Survival Techniques	40	The Ocean's Depths	56
Wild Migrations	42	Did You Know?	58
Animal Awards	44	Glossary	60
Ever-Changing Forests	46	Index	61
Life in the Rainforest	48		
Survival in the Desert	50		
Untamed Arctic Tundra	52		
Lively Fresh Water	54		

What Is Nature?

Nature is everything around us that hasn't been made by humans. From the rocks and sand we walk on, to the animals and plants that grow, and the weather that we experience – it's all part of nature!

Find the balance

Plants, animals, and weather work together to keep our world healthy and full of life. Everything needs to be balanced for nature to thrive.

Across the world

Our planet is made up of lots of **habitats**, which have their own features and living things. This means nature looks different around the world.

Planet Earth

Our planet is very special – it has the right conditions for life to exist. In fact, scientists think Earth is the only planet with living things!

Ocean and land

Most of Earth's surface is covered in water! It's sometimes called the "Blue Planet" because of how it looks from outer space.

Crust

Mantle

Outer core

Inner core

Shining Sun

The Sun is a ball of hot **gas** that Earth is always moving around. It's the reason Earth has heat, light, and **nutrients** – things all plants and animals need to live.

Deep layers

Hidden under Earth's surface are thick layers of rock and metal, which get hotter the deeper they are. The deepest part is thought to be as hot as the surface of the Sun!

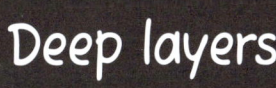

Make Your Own Earth

Always ask an adult to help when using scissors and sharp objects.

You will need:

- Six pieces of paper: blue, green, brown, red, orange, and yellow.
- Scissors
- Glue
- Paper fastener

1. Cut out two big circles from the brown and blue paper. Then cut out red, orange, and yellow circles, each smaller than the last.

2. Cut out shapes of the land from the green paper. Glue them onto the blue circle and cut out a quarter.

3. Layer the brown, red, orange, yellow, and blue circles as shown, and secure with the paper fastener. Your Earth with its layers is complete!

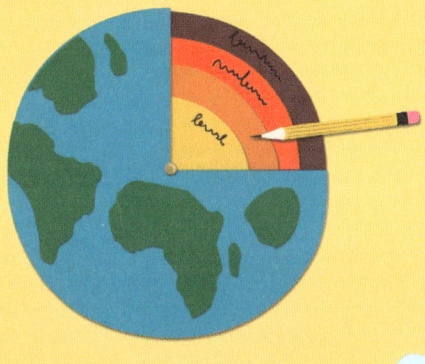

Moving Surfaces

Earth's surface – the crust – is split into giant pieces called tectonic plates. These plates are always moving, which can cause natural disasters and is the reason we have different landscapes.

Mighty mountains

When tectonic plates push into each other, the ground can rise into mountains. Volcanoes are mountains that sometimes erupt, shooting out hot **lava**!

New land

When volcanoes erupt in the ocean, something amazing happens! When the lava touches the water, it cools and hardens into solid rock, creating new land.

Earthquakes and tsunamis

Earthquakes are also caused by Earth's tectonic plates moving. These shakes come from deep underground but can be strong enough for us to feel! Big earthquakes sometimes cause huge waves called tsunamis.

Under the Surface

Rocks under the ground's surface hold lots of secrets about Earth's history, including plants and animals that lived on Earth long before humans!

Fascinating fossils

Fossils are remains of living things that have been preserved in rock for millions of years. Bones and shells are common fossils. They help us learn about things that are no longer around, like dinosaurs!

Ancient rocks

There are many types of rock. They are made of different **minerals**, which affects how they look. Over time, rocks stack in layers, hiding clues about what the world and its **climate** was like long ago.

Fishy finds

Sometimes scientists find fossils of **aquatic** animals really far from the ocean! This tells us some places that are land today used to be underwater. The natural world has changed a lot over time.

What's Hidden Inside Rocks?

Rocks are made of different minerals and metals. These materials can be collected and used to create many beautiful and useful items.

Gold
One of the world's most expensive metals, gold is often turned into rings, bracelets, and necklaces.

Silver
This shiny metal is used to make trophies, coins, and cutlery.

Sand
Sand is made from rocks that have broken down into tiny pieces over thousands or millions of years.

Amethyst
These purple crystals are cut and polished into shining gemstones, to be used in rings and necklaces.

Ruby
Rubies are among the rarest gemstones. They range from red to pink, with dark red being the most popular.

Quartz
Tiny quartz crystals are found in many of Earth's rocks, but the world's largest are bigger than a person!

Graphite and diamond
Graphite and diamond are both made of **carbon**, but they look very different! Diamonds are valuable and used in rings, but graphite is used in pencils!

The Water Cycle

All living things need water to survive. Our planet's water moves from rivers and oceans to the clouds and back again in a cycle that has been happening for more than 4 billion years!

1. Evaporation

Heated by the Sun, water in rivers and oceans turn into tiny droplets that rise into the air.

2. Condensation

Then, high in the sky, the water droplets cool down and stick together to form clouds.

3. Precipitation

When clouds get very heavy, the water droplets fall back to the ground as rain, hail, or snow.

4. Collection

Plants and rivers collect water that runs into the soil or ocean. Then the water cycle begins again!

World of cycles

The water cycle isn't the only cycle in nature. Rocks and nutrients are also recycled and play an important part in helping the natural world stay healthy.

Beyond Earth

Nature stretches beyond Earth too. It goes deep into outer space and includes all the other moons, stars, and planets. The whole universe is interconnected!

waxing gibbous

First quarter

Waxing crescent

New moon

Shooting stars
These bright streaks shooting across the sky are actually meteors – rocks from outer space. Many of them are as old as our solar system!

Shining constellations

Constellations are groups of stars that form shapes or pictures in the night sky. They may look close together, but they are actually huge distances apart.

Full moon

Waning gibbous

Last quarter

Waning crescent

Moon phases

The Moon doesn't make its own light – moonlight is really sunlight bouncing off its surface! As the Moon **orbits** Earth, it seems to change shape, but this is only a clever mix of sunlight and shadows.

How Plants Grow

Plants come in all shapes and sizes, from tiny flowers to towering trees. But no matter how they look, all plants need a few important things to grow: nutrients, space, air, water, and sunlight.

Nutrients
Plants use their roots to collect the nutrients and water they need to grow from the soil.

Roots

Space
Some plants need space around them, so they don't have to compete with other plants for nutrients and sunlight.

Water and air
Like us, plants also need plenty of water and air to survive. Without them, plants would shrivel up!

Sunlight
Plants turn light from the Sun into food, which gives them energy to grow.

Grow Your Own Cress

Cress can be used in salads and cooking.

You will need:
- Cotton wool
- A clean, small plastic pot
- Water and spray bottle
- Cress seeds
- Scissors

1. Wet some cotton wool and place it in the bottom of the plastic pot.

2. Sprinkle a teaspoon of cress seeds onto the wet cotton wool and press down gently.

3. Place the pot in a warm, light place. Spray the seeds with a little water every day to keep them moist.

4. Once your cress has reached 4 inches (10 cm), ask an adult to chop off the top so you can eat it. Yum!

Ancient Plants

Plants are some of the oldest living things on the planet! They've survived ice ages, towered over dinosaurs, and outlived whole groups of people.

Cladoxylopsida (cla-doh-zil-op-sih-duh)

Thought to have been the first trees ever, these plants grew more than 370 million years ago! They were related to modern-day ferns.

Monkey puzzle tree

These **evergreen** trees have been around for 200 million years. Scientists think they were the food of long-necked plant-eating dinosaurs like Diplodocus.

Archaefructus (ar-kee-fruk-tus)

This aquatic plant is thought to be one of the world's oldest flowering plants. It has been studied from fossils that date back 125 million years.

Narrow-leafed campion

This little flower is a record-breaker. It became the oldest prehistoric plant brought back to life when scientists grew it from seeds that were more than 30,000 years old!

Wollemi pine tree

People thought these pine trees became **extinct** 2 million years ago. Then, in the 1990s, a small number were found growing in Australia!

Hard fern

Ferns are among the oldest land plants. The earliest ferns, which lived at the same time as the dinosaurs, are only known from fossils. But there are still thousands of **species** growing today.

Tree Communication

Trees may look silent and lonely, but they may have clever ways of working together. Some scientists even think trees work with other living things!

A helping hand

Scientists believe some trees send signals to warn other trees about dangers like **drought** and **disease**! It's possible they also share nutrients with young, old, or sick trees to help them grow.

Wildlife teamwork

The secret of trees' teamwork may be hidden underground, where **fungi** connect roots together. Some scientists think fungi help trees share signals and resources in exchange for nutrients!

Amazing Plant Adaptations

Plants around the world **adapt** to cope with the climate and other plants or animals in their surroundings. Some adaptations are really impressive!

Maple tree
In hot weather, trees like maple drop their leaves in order to save precious water and energy.

Stone pine
To survive in fire-prone areas, some trees, like the stone pine, grow really thick **bark** and super tall **crowns**. This keeps their important parts safe.

Deadly nightshade
Many plants grow **poisonous** fruit, but every part of deadly nightshade can be deadly! Very few animals survive after eating it, so many have learned to stay away.

What Am I?

Nature is full of incredible tricksters disguising themselves as something they're not. Can you guess which of these are plants and which are animals?

Coral
Growing on rocks in the ocean, coral looks like a plant, but it's actually made up of tiny animals that build hard skeletons and become giant reefs.

Sea sponge
Spongy, soft, and unmoving, you may think sea sponges are plants, but they're actually ocean animals! They've been around for millions of years.

Hummingbird

Green birdflower
This may look just like a green hummingbird, but it's actually a flower! This plant belongs to the same family as peas.

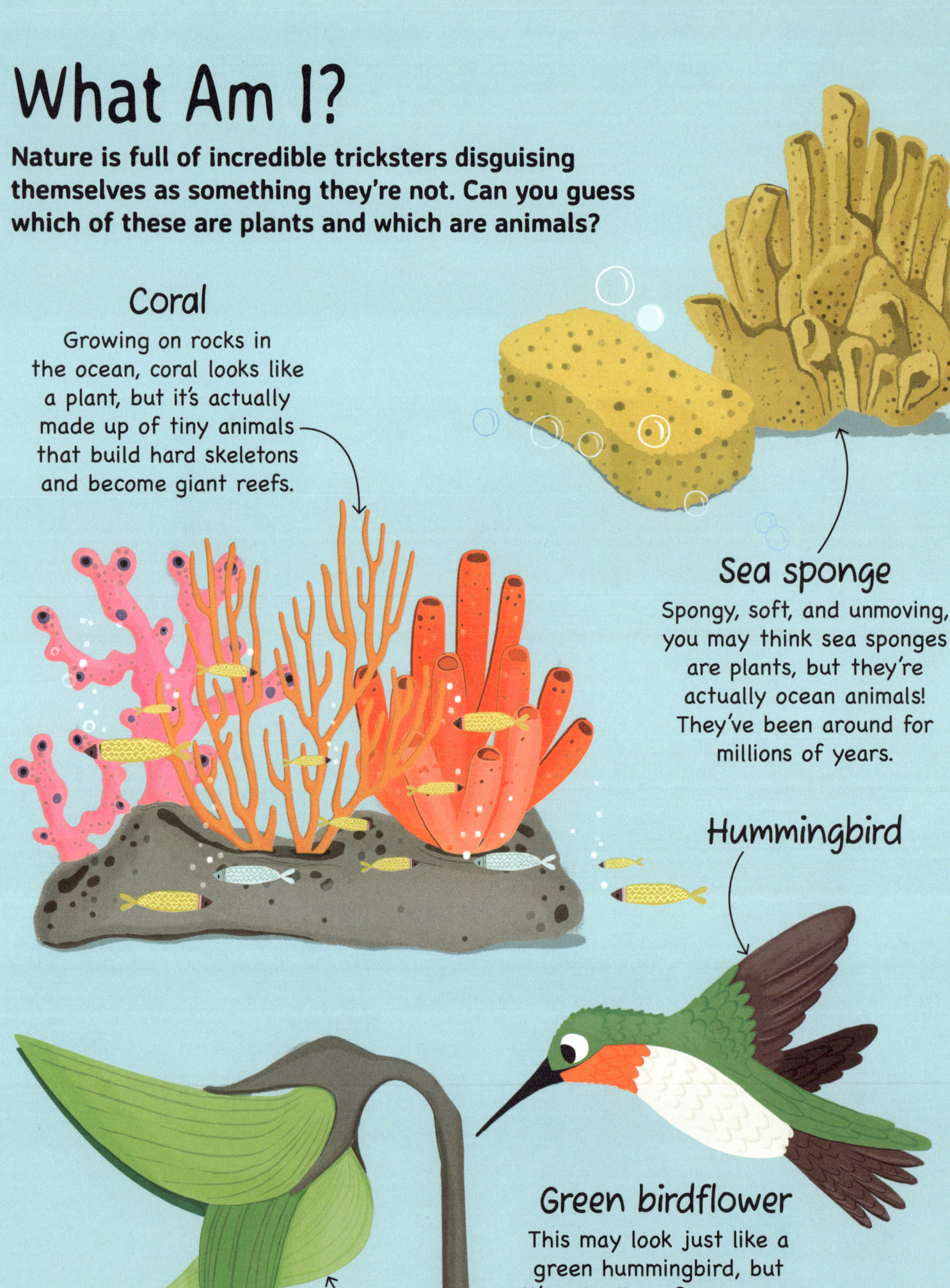

Monkey-faced orchid
This look-alike rainforest flower could be easily mistaken for a monkey. It's thought this might stop real monkeys from eating it!

Bunny succulent
With tiny rabbit-shaped tops, this plant has the cutest disguise of all. While naturally found in hot places, bunny succulents also make good houseplants!

Mushrooms
Mushrooms may look and act like plants, but they're not. And they're not animals either! They are actually a type of fungi.

Keeping the Planet Healthy

Whether on land or in the ocean, plants do lots of incredible things to help the natural world stay balanced and healthy.

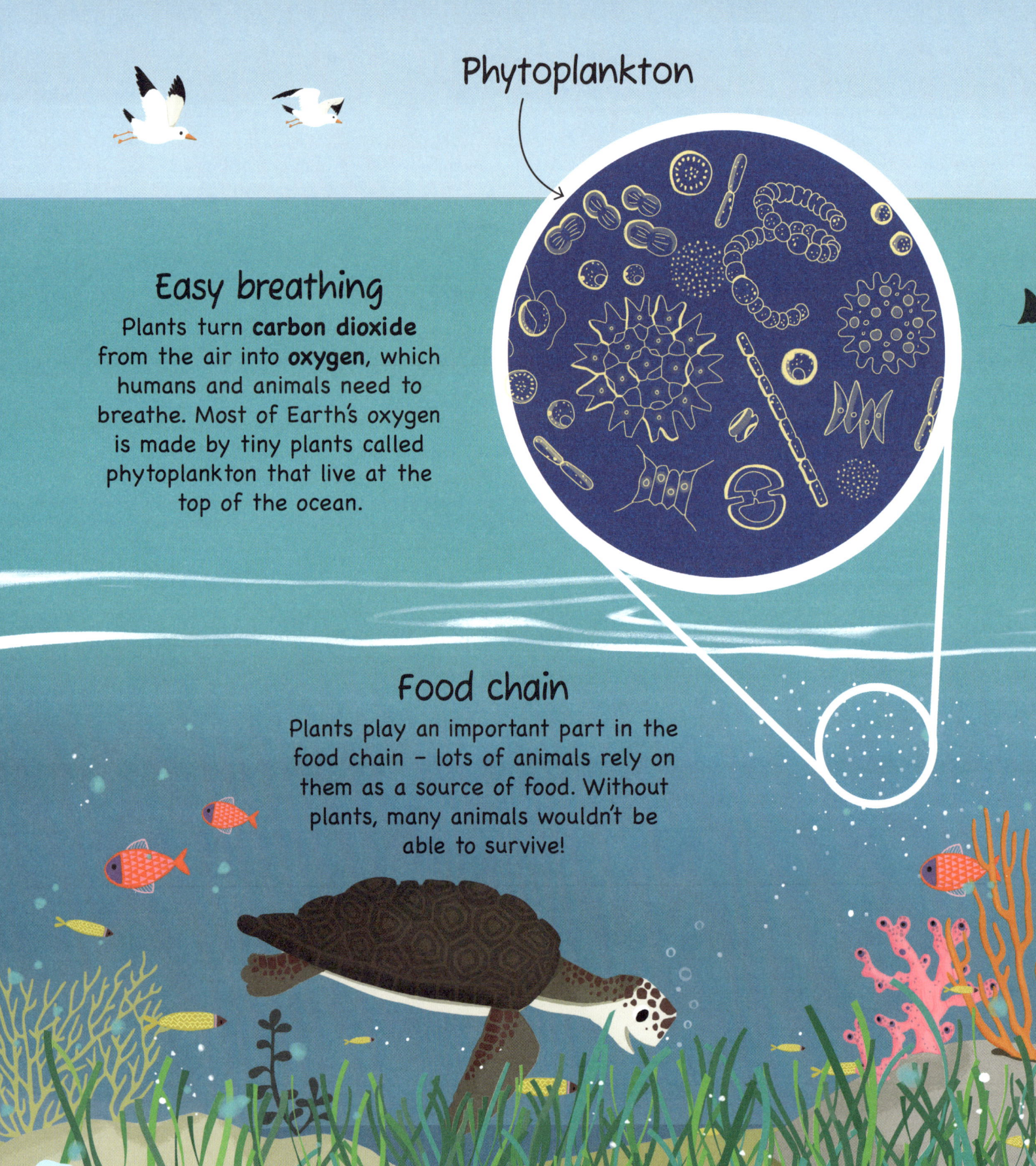

Phytoplankton

Easy breathing

Plants turn **carbon dioxide** from the air into **oxygen**, which humans and animals need to breathe. Most of Earth's oxygen is made by tiny plants called phytoplankton that live at the top of the ocean.

Food chain

Plants play an important part in the food chain – lots of animals rely on them as a source of food. Without plants, many animals wouldn't be able to survive!

Pollution fighters

Trees take in **pollution** from the air, water, and soil, keeping the environment clean for all the living things that call Earth home. Their cleaning efforts help to keep **global warming** at bay.

Animal habitats

Trees and plants provide safety for lots of animals, who use them as shelter or to make their homes. Animals help plants out too by spreading seeds and scaring off plant-eating pests.

Types of Animals

There are millions of different animals in the world, but most of them fit into a few main groups based on their body features and how they live.

Amphibians

Amphibians are soft-skinned animals that start their lives in water, hatching from eggs. They grow to breathe air and live on land. Frogs, toads, and newts are all amphibians.

Mammals

Cows, dogs, and humans are all mammals — warm-blooded animals with hair or fur that give birth to live babies, not eggs. Mammals make milk for their babies too.

Birds

Birds are the only animals with feathers! They also have wings and beaks, and many of them can fly.

Reptiles

Crocodiles, snakes, and lizards are reptiles – animals with dry, scaly skin that can live on land or in water.

Fish

Fish live in water. They have fins, tails, and gills, which are like special lungs that allow them to breathe underwater!

Clever Animal Adaptations

Just like plants, animals can change their appearance or habits to suit their habitats, help them catch food, or to avoid becoming food themselves!

Smooth movers

Body parts like long claws and tails aren't just for hunting – they help animals climb, jump, and balance as they move through the wild.

Deadly poison

Many animals use poison to defend themselves from **predators**. A poison dart frog's bright skin warns other animals to keep their distance!

Smart hunters

The smartest hunters sneak up on **prey** with no warning! Pelicans swoop down from above, using their big beaks to catch fish by surprise.

Mobile homes

Some animals, including crabs, have hard shells that protect their soft insides from hungry predators. Some can completely hide inside their shells if needed!

Clever camouflage

Animals like flat fish can make themselves almost invisible! Changing their skin to look like the things around them is a clever survival skill.

Incredible Insects

Insects may be small, but they can do some amazing things!

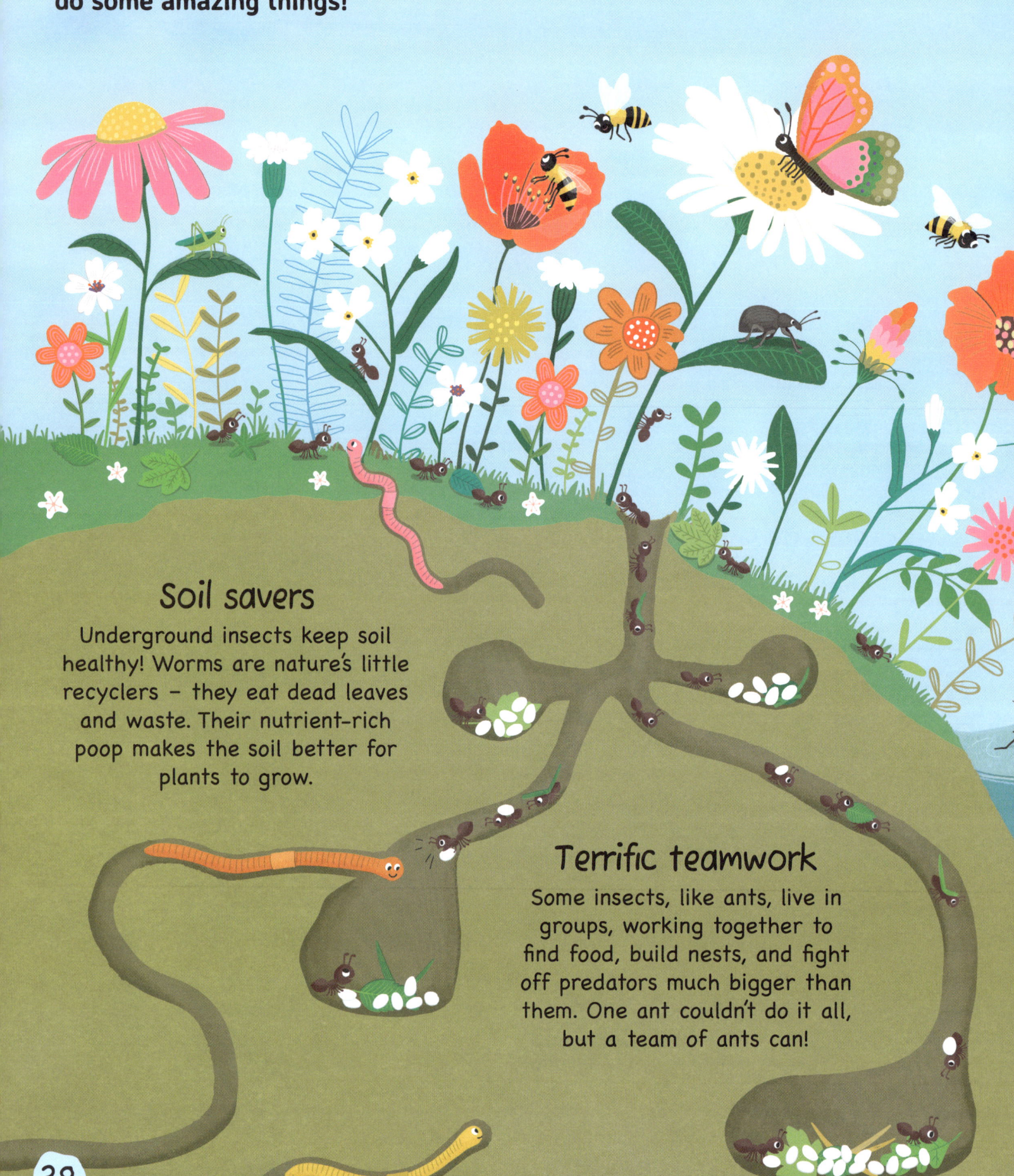

Soil savers

Underground insects keep soil healthy! Worms are nature's little recyclers – they eat dead leaves and waste. Their nutrient-rich poop makes the soil better for plants to grow.

Terrific teamwork

Some insects, like ants, live in groups, working together to find food, build nests, and fight off predators much bigger than them. One ant couldn't do it all, but a team of ants can!

Plant friends

Lots of insects, like bees and butterflies, are great for plants. As they visit flowers in search of food, they spread **pollen**, helping plants make fruit and seeds so more plants can grow!

Grow Your Own Worm Food

You will need:
- Fallen leaves
- Netting (from an old fruit or vegetable sack)
- Tent stakes
- Notebook
- Pencil/pen

1. Pick a spot outside with thick grass and soft soil. Lay out some fallen leaves in a pile on the ground.

2. Cover the leaf pile with netting, using tent stakes to hold it in place. In your notebook, draw the pile of leaves as they are and write "Start" underneath.

3. Check the leaf pile the next week to see if any leaves have been eaten! Draw the pile of leaves as they are now and write "Week one" underneath.

4. Keep checking on your leaf pile to watch it change over time as the hungry worms come back again and again for a meal!

Survival Techniques

The natural world is a dangerous place. Animals have to be very clever to survive!

It's dinnertime!

Just like us, animals eat different things. Carnivores only eat meat, herbivores only eat plants, but omnivores eat both, so they can always find something to eat!

Staying in touch

Animals communicate for different reasons, including to warn others about danger or mark their **territory**. Some use sound, like howling, while others use smell or touch.

Awake all night

Nocturnal animals sleep by day and are awake at night! It's easier to sneak up on prey in the dark. Plus, being nocturnal helps animals cope in habitats that get very hot during the day.

Safety in numbers

Many animals, like zebras, live in big groups to stay safe from predators. But hyenas live in groups too, working together to hunt prey!

Teamwork

Lots of animals team up with each other. Oxpecker birds land on rhinos and eat bugs off their skin. It's great food for the birds and keeps the rhinos clean.

Wild Migrations

Animals don't always stay in one place. Some may need to flee disaster, others **migrate**, completing the same journey between two places every year.

Better weather

Arctic tern birds may be small, but their migration is the longest of all! They travel from the Arctic to the Antarctic to experience two summers every year.

Finding food

Reindeer have the longest land migration. Every spring they migrate north in huge herds, in search of food to eat and safer places to have their babies.

Changing journey

Migrating animals help plants by spreading seeds and pollen. But global warming is making animals migrate at different times and to different places, affecting both animals and plants.

Having babies

Even some insects migrate! Monarch butterflies travel in search of warmer places where it's better for the females to lay their eggs.

Animal Awards

These record-breaking animals are some of the most impressive.

Oldest land animal
The oldest known land animal is a Seychelles giant tortoise called Jonathan who is more than 190 years old!

Tallest animal
Giraffes are the tallest animals in the world. They have incredibly long legs and necks, which means they grow to be around 18 feet (5.5 m) tall.

Biggest animal
Blue whales are thought to be the biggest animals in the world ever – even bigger than the biggest dinosaur was!

Strongest animal

The African bush elephant is the strongest animal. It's able to lift around 19,800 lbs (9,000 kg) which is the same as four cars at once!

Sleepiest animal

Koalas sleep between 18 and 22 hours per day! Their leafy diet doesn't give them much energy, so they need lots of sleep.

Ever-Changing Forests

Planet Earth's habitats are home to a unique combination of plants and animals. Temperate forests are large areas that are covered in trees.

Changing seasons

Many temperate forests experience seasons, with hot, sunny summers and cold, snowy winters. This means the forest looks very different at different times of the year.

Buzzing with life

Forest plants and animals are all connected. From birds nesting in trees to bees spreading pollen, everything helps keep the habitat balanced.

Sleepy forest

To survive the winter, some plants become **dormant**, dropping their leaves to save energy. Similarly, some animals hibernate, reappearing in the spring when it's warmer.

Beautiful greenery

Some trees don't lose their leaves in winter! These trees, called evergreens, usually have needles or scales instead of flat, wide leaves.

Life in the Rainforest

These mysterious, tropical habitats are home to around half of the planet's known plant and animal species! They are thick, hot, and exotic.

Water everywhere!

As the name suggests, rainforests get a lot of rain! With so many plants growing close together, and lots of rivers and wet soil, the air stays damp all the time.

48

Saving the day

Rainforests are full of incredible plants, many of which we collect to eat and even to turn into powerful, life-saving medicines!

Flowers

The flowers that grow here are usually bright and smelly to attract pollinators. Many grow on vines that climb trees to reach sunlight, while others adapt to the dim forest floor.

Trees

Rainforests are full of trees competing for resources. They grow incredibly tall to reach sunlight and have big, shallow roots to grab what little nutrients are in the soil.

Animals

The rainforest is so dark and thick, predators could be anywhere! To stay safe, animals become great at climbing or flying quickly, or use camouflage or poison.

49

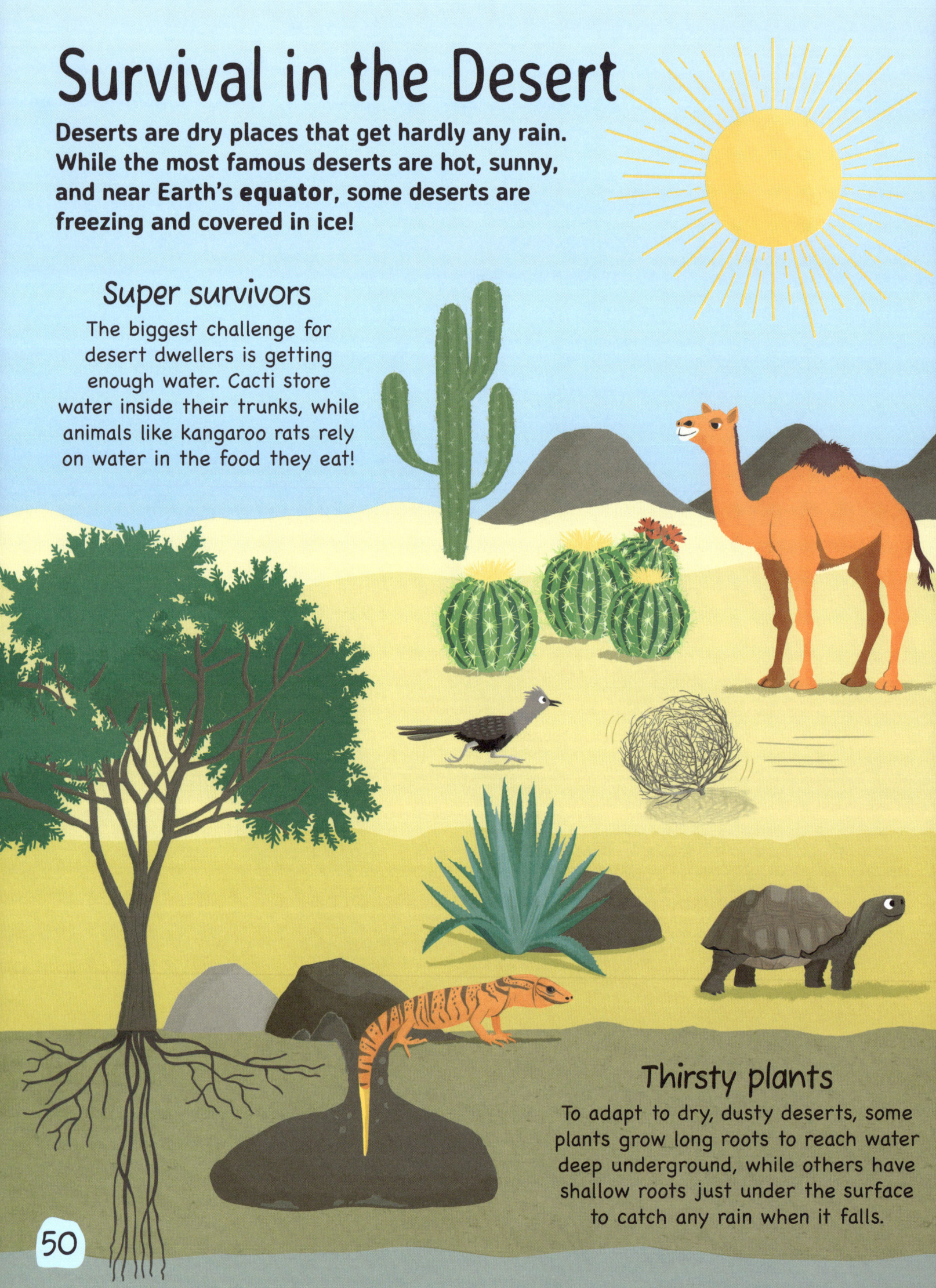

Survival in the Desert

Deserts are dry places that get hardly any rain. While the most famous deserts are hot, sunny, and near Earth's **equator**, some deserts are freezing and covered in ice!

Super survivors

The biggest challenge for desert dwellers is getting enough water. Cacti store water inside their trunks, while animals like kangaroo rats rely on water in the food they eat!

Thirsty plants

To adapt to dry, dusty deserts, some plants grow long roots to reach water deep underground, while others have shallow roots just under the surface to catch any rain when it falls.

Clear skies

With few trees, deserts are hit by strong winds. Lots of wind but little rain means there are no clouds, making hot deserts blazing hot by day and really cold at night!

Busy night

To survive extreme temperatures, many desert animals are nocturnal, hiding underground during the day. Some flowers, like the Queen of the Night, only bloom at night!

Kangaroo rat

Untamed Arctic Tundra

One of the coldest habitats, the Arctic tundra is similar to a cold desert – it's bitter, dry, and a difficult place for things to live!

Harsh soil

The tundra is so cold that most water is trapped as ice. Most of the soil is frozen too! Only a few small plants with short roots can survive in this harsh place.

Top of the world

The Arctic tundra is far north and surrounds the Arctic circle. In summer, it has weeks of nonstop daylight – the Sun never goes down! In winter, nights last for weeks as the Sun never rises!

Arctic fox

Arctic ground squirrel

Coping with extremes

Some animals, like Arctic ground squirrels, hibernate in winter to cope when food and water is in short supply. Others, like Arctic foxes, use amazing hearing and camouflage to sneak up on prey – they're great hunters.

Go with the flow

Waterways like streams and rivers almost always run into the ocean. Sometimes they start as snow on mountains. Water travels a long way!

Animal helpers

Heavy rain can have a huge impact on these habitats by causing floods! Beavers help by building dams, which redirect water and protect the area.

Dam

Swampy situation

Swamps are wetlands that are full of trees. Their water levels change often, so only the well-adapted, like trees with special roots, survive!

The Ocean's Depths

The largest habitat of all, Earth's oceans are divided into layers, which are each home to different living things. The deepest layer is still mostly unexplored.

Shining through
The ocean's top layer is the only one that gets sunlight, which is why it's the only layer where plants grow!

Don't hold your breath
All animals breathe oxygen, even those that live underwater! Most fish get to oxygen from water, but mammals like whales need to swim to the surface for air.

Calm below the storm

Storms and waves only affect the ocean's surface. Deep waters stay calm but have higher **pressure**, which is a different challenge to cope with!

Life in the dark

The ocean is deeper than the height of Mount Everest! Its depths are pitch black, so many animals living there are bioluminescent – they glow and create their own light!

Did You Know?

Our natural world is very special; it's home to millions of living things, which all rely on each other to survive. So there's lots of reasons to protect our planet! Did you know these amazing facts about nature?

Amphibians, like frogs, absorb water **AND POLLUTION** through their skin!

Rainforest trees **CLEAN THE AIR AND WATER,** which helps keep the climate stable.

Seagrass meadows provide **FOOD AND SHELTER** for many ocean animals.

Glossary

Adapt – (verb) when a living thing develops special features or skills to help it survive in its environment.

Aquatic – something that grows, lives, or spends a lot of time in water.

Bark – the tough outer layer of a woody plant stem or root, such as a tree trunk.

Carbon – a natural element found inside all living things, the air, and rocks.

Carbon dioxide – an invisible gas in the air that plants take in to make food and oxygen.

Climate – long-term temperatures and weather conditions.

Crowns – the top part of the tree which has the branches and leaves.

Disease – illness; a condition that can harm living things.

Dormant – living things that are alive but not currently growing.

Drought – an unusually long period of dryness, usually caused by lack of rainfall.

Equator – an invisible line around the middle of Earth, an equal distance from the North and South poles. It's usually very hot there.

Evergreen – a type of plant that keeps its leaves and stays green all year round.

Extinct – when a species no longer exists.

Fresh water – water that is naturally not salty, for example rainwater.

Fungi – (the plural of fungus). A group of living things, including mushrooms, molds/moulds, and yeasts, that are neither plants nor animals.

Gas – a substance, like air, that spreads out to fill any space. Most gases are invisible.

Global warming – the rising temperature of the planet over time, which can cause problems for nature.

Habitats – the natural homes of plants and animals.

Lava – hot, melted rock that has come from underground.

Migrate – (verb) when animals move from one place to another, usually to find food or better weather.

Minerals – substances that are naturally found in things like rocks, sand, and soil.

Nutrients – substances or ingredients that plants and animals need to live and grow.

Orbits – (verb) to circle around another object in outer space.

Oxygen – an invisible gas in the air that plants produce, and people and animals breathe.

Poisonous – something that is very harmful and can cause severe illness or death.

Pollen – a dusty powder made by some plants. When moved between different flowers, it helps plants make new seeds.

Pollution – harmful substances or materials in an environment.

Predators – animals that hunt other animals.

Pressure – the force of something pushing down from above.

Prey – animals that are hunted by other animals.

Species – a group of living things that are the same as each other. For example, Douglas fir and noble fir trees are two different tree species.

Territory – an area that belongs to, or is controlled by something or someone.

Unique – something that is one of its kind; unlike all others.

Index

A
Activities 11, 23, 39
Ancient plants 24-25
Animals 8, 14-15, 24-25, 29, 30-31,
　　　32-33, 34-35, 36-37, 38-39, 40-41,
　　　42-43, 44-45, 46-47, 48-49, 50-51,
　　　52-53, 54-55, 56-57, 58-59
Aquatic habitats 15, 54-55, 56-57

C
Cacti 29, 50
Climate 15, 28, 33, 43, 58, 60

D
Dangerous plants 28
Dinosaurs 14-15, 24-25, 44

E
Earthquakes 13
Extreme environments
　　　Arctic tundra 52-53
　　　Desert 29, 50-51
　　　Rainforest 29, 31, 48-49, 58
　　　Swamp 54-55

F
Ferns 24-25
Flowers 22, 24-25, 29, 30-31, 39, 49,
　　　51, 59
Forests 46-47
Fossils 14-15, 24-25
Fruit 28-29, 39
Fungi 26-27, 31, 60

G
Gemstones 17
Global warming 33, 43, 60
Grass 58

H
Hibernation 47, 53

I
Insects 38-39, 41, 43

M
Medicine 49
Metals 11, 16
Migration 42-43, 60
Minerals 15, 16, 60
Moon 20-21
Mountains 12-13, 55

N
Nocturnal species 41, 51
Nutrients 11, 19, 22, 26, 29, 38, 49,
　　　54, 59, 60

O
Outer space 10-11, 20-21

P
Plants 8, 14, 19, 22-23, 24-25,
　　　26-27, 28-29, 30-31, 32-33,
　　　38-39, 40, 46-47, 48-49,
　　　50-51, 52-53, 54-55, 56,
　　　58-59
Pollen 39, 43, 46, 60
Pollution 33, 58, 60

R
Rocks 8, 11, 13, 14-15, 16-17, 19,
　　　20, 30

S
Seeds 25, 29, 33, 38, 43
Soil 19, 22, 29, 33, 38
Sun 11, 18, 21, 22-23, 29, 46, 49,
　　　50, 53, 56, 59

T
Trees 22, 24-25, 26-27, 28-29,
　　　33, 46-47, 49, 51, 55
Tsunamis 13

V
Volcanoes 12-13

W
Water cycle 18-19
Weather 8, 28, 42, 55
Wood wide web 27

61